THE POST-WAR FINANCIAL REHABILITATION OF THE NETHERLANDS

The Post-War Financial Rehabilitation of The Netherlands

by

P. LIEFTINCK

MARTINUS NIJHOFF — THE HAGUE

1973

Softcover reprint of the hardcover 1st edition 1973

ISBN 978-94-011-8700-8 ISBN 978-94-011-9524-9 (eBook)
DOI 10.1007/978-94-011-9524-9

CONTENTS

INTRODUCTION

Economic and political background

When after five years of war and occupation (May 1940–May 1945) The Netherlands started on the road to recovery, the economy was in a catastrophic condition. As a result of destruction, requisitioning and looting, and of unavoidable expenditures by the Government in exile, the national wealth in terms of real and financial assets had been reduced by about 30 per cent. The productive capacity in industry, agriculture, transportation and infrastructure was heavily damaged, stocks were exhausted and labor productivity was seriously underminded (the daily food ration had reached the near-starvation level of barely 600 calories per person).[1] Monetary reserves and foreign investments had suffered heavy losses.

The economic and social strategy on which the new post-war Government embarked was directed towards three major objectives: a) rapid reconstruction of the productive potential; b) equitable distribution of the national income; c) rational utilization of the available economic resources. It was realized that the achievement of these objectives was conditioned by austerity with respect to consumption, after a reasonable subsistence level had been restored; by a maximum investment effort; by the re-establish-

[1] During the war period, the population had increased by more than 400,000 reaching 9.3 million end-1945.

ment and maintenance of internal and external financial stability combined with a high level of employment; by the fullest possible participation in international trade; and by a broadly acceptable sharing of the burden of material loss suffered during the war, a correction of flagrant income disparities, and an improvement of the social security system.

Against this brief general background, this paper deals with the post-war financial rehabilitation and stabilization of the Netherlands. It concentrates on the monetary and fiscal policies and performance during the years 1945-1952 in the broader framework of the country's economic recovery. The primary purpose is to illustrate the role played by the adjustment of money supply to the level and growth of national income, and the paper is presented as a case history of combatting inflation under extraordinary circumstances and with rather unconventional methods.

The excess of money

At the time of liberation, the danger of a runaway inflation was imminent. Whereas inventories were depleted, the volume of domestic production had dropped to one third of that in 1938 and import capacity was greatly impaired both physically and financially; yet the money supply was more than four times as high as in 1938. This large increase in the money supply had two main causes. Firstly, exports (partly forced) of goods and services, and of Government securities held by Dutch investors to Germany during the occupation resulted in large balance of payments surpluses. These were settled in Reichsmarks which were presented for conversion into guilders with the Netherlands Bank (the central bank of The Netherlands) adding an amount of about 6 billion guilders to the currency in circulation. Secondly, increasing budget deficits fed by high occupation costs were financed through the banking system by placing Treasury bills with the commercial banks (the money revolving via the budget), or directly with the central bank. This financing of the public deficit caused a large increase in sight deposits with the banks that was only partly offset by the decrease in bank credit to the private sector resulting from the decline in business activity. On balance, this accounted for an additional increase in the money supply of well over 2 billion guilders. In May 1945 the total money supply (coins, notes and sight deposits) amounted to 10,908 million guilders, as compared with 2,640 million guilders five years earlier.

According to a rough estimate the national income (at market prices) had dropped from 5,400 million guilders in 1938 to an estimated level of 3,000 million guilders in May 1945. Despite the disparity between the changes in national income and the volume of money, as a result of price and wage controls and rationing of all first necessities the official index of wholesale prices was at that time around 80 percent, the cost of living around 60 per cent, and wages around 40 per cent, above the pre-war level. But black market prices had soared sky high. With the return of a national Government followed by the arrival of some emergency food supplies, rumors spread about a forthcoming invalidation of banknotes. In fact, on July 9th, 1945, as a first measure against hoarding of money made in the black market, all 100 guilder notes were withdrawn from circulation.[2] Subject to a brief time limit, the facility was opened for holders of such notes, upon their delivery to a domestic bank, to be credited for the amount on a blocked account. Actually, a number of holders shrank from doing so and some others failed the deadline. Stimulated by these events, and encouraged by an appeal from the Government, many holders of banknotes of smaller denominations voluntarily deposited large amounts of these with various banking institutions. Consequently,

[2] Banknotes of large denominations (500 and 1,000 guilders) had already been invalidated in March 1943 by the occupying authorities.

the total circulation of banknotes declined from 4,901 million guilders on July 9th to 1,863 million guilders on September 24th, 1945. The counterpart was a rapid increase in sight deposits, so that despite a change in its composition, the overall volume of money remained far in excess of normal during the summer of 1945.

The dangers ahead

This situation, together with the uncertainty about further measures in respect of money, created a climate harmful to a resumption of normal working habits and presented an acute threat of runaway inflation which could not be contained effectively by a continuation of price and wage controls and rationing only. Operators in the black market enjoyed a heyday, farmers were reluctant to sell their crops, traders shunned money and stored up goods, valuables of all kinds brought high premiums, coins were hoarded. Fearful of being trapped if the rumors of a forthcoming screening of all money holdings were to come true, people began to invest their cash in a variety of secondary instruments of liquid assets (postal and social security stamps, checks, letters of credit, Treasury paper and the like) or to make advance payments, hoping thereby to evade control. At the same time, these manipulations caused the money to be spread among a wider group of the population.

Given the character of the Dutch, there was a strong and general psychological urge to return as quickly as possible to a normal pattern of working, earning, saving and spending supported by confidence in the value of the money based on its relative scarcity. It was felt also that the distribution of liquid assets had become greatly distorted and that it would be intolerable, when supplies of commodities improved, if those who happened to be in a strong liquid position (which rightly or wrongly created suspicion of war-profiteering) would be able to satisfy their needs at the expense of the large majority of the population with only meager money reserves and suffering from manifold losses. This did not apply only to the acquisition of scarce consumer goods, but also to meeting much needed investments in household commodities, stocks and equipment goods. An additional factor of concern for the autorities was the tension that competitive spending between the private and public sectors was bound to create in the allocation of scarce national resources under conditions of continued abundant liquidity in private hands. The economic and social priorities set by the Government could not be allowed to be put in jeopardy, and these required not only stability and avoidance of inflation, but also a firm grip on the pattern of spending, both internally and externally.

It took the new Government, which came into office at the end of June 1945, three months to complete its preparations for the execution of a comprehensive stabilisation and reconstruction program. The main technical constraint in the monetary field was the time required to manufacture a sufficient quantity of new banknotes and Treasury notes, which it was intended to put into circulation in adequate amounts to substitute for the existing paper money. As soon as this condition was fulfilled, which was by the end of September, the programme of the so-called 'Monetary Campaign' was launched, and herewith began the first phase of the financial rehabilitation of the country.

THE MONETARY PURGE AND THE PERIOD OF SUPPRESSED INFLATION, 1945–1948

The monetary purge

The first measure taken in the financial field was the monetary purge of September 26, 1945. This consisted of the withdrawal of all currency in circulation (banknotes and Treasury notes) with the exception of coins, and the blocking of all deposit money (sight deposits and others) in the banks, followed by the issuance of new currency and the deblocking of bank accounts, after screening, in such amounts as to allow the money supply gradually to expand in accordance with the real growth of the economy.

This measure was intended to serve three objectives. The first was to bring into the open all money and near-money holdings, in particular those improperly acquired during the years of foreign occupation by collaboration with the enemy and operations in the black market. The existing bank secret was abolished. Currency notes not turned in to authorized institutions lost its validity. The second was to register all liquid assets in the form of money and near-money holdings for the purpose of tax assessment under the existing tax legislation and the special reconstruction taxes that were going to be imposed. The third and most important objective was to re-establish an appropriate relationship between the quantity of goods available and the supply of money in circulation.

The achievement of the third and main objective took, understandably, several months. To serve the minimum payments needs of the first week following the currency withdrawal and the blockade of bank deposits, new banknotes were made available in an amount of 10 guilders per head of the population, and by the end of the week sufficient additional money was released to finance the income earned over that period. This release was continued for some time until the money supply had filled the national payments circuit. Special releases were authorized to meet normal requirements of enterprises for working capital and exceptional needs for rehabilitation and emergencies that could not be paid out of current income. New bank credit was originally permitted only after the applicant had obtained release of his blocked account; later this provision was dropped, although all new credit remained subject to licensing for a considerable length of time. By the end of 1945 the ratio between national income and the amount of money in circulation in the form of coins, banknotes, and Treasury notes and freely disposable bank deposits had almost returned to its prewar level. (See Table I).

With respect to the remaining surplus of monetary claims held on blocked accounts, five options were opened:

(1) continuation of these holdings on blocked account in the hope and expectation of future releases;

(2) transfer of limited amounts to a medium-term savings account;

(3) use of these holdings for payment of tax arrears incurred during the occupation;

(4) use of these holdings to fulfill obligations in respect to the new special reconstruction taxes to be imposed;

(5) subscription to long-term, low-interest bearing Goverment loans.

By far the most use was made of the last three options which meant that the bulk of the surplus landed into the Government Treasury, where it was held and only gradually released for public spending according to the growing needs connected with the rehabilitation of the economy.

Table I *Money Supply and National Income*
(in millions of guilders)

	Money Supply[1] (12 months' average)	National Income (market prices)	Percentage of Money Supply to National Income
1938	2,480[2]	5,400[3]	46
1945 (May)	10,908	3,000[4]	300–400[4]
1945 (Dec.)	4,100	8,000[4]	51[4]
1946	5,410	9,930	54
1947	6,470	12,070	54
1948	7,190	14,230	51
1949	7,337	15,960	46
1950	7,267	17,750	41
1951	6,984	19,560	36
1952	7,687	20,170	38

[1] Coins, notes and sight deposits.
[2] Average at the beginning and end of the year.
[3] The year 1938 was a severe depression year with large unemployment.
[4] Estimated level.

Sources: Annual Reports of the Netherlands Bank, 1947–1954.
White Paper on Monetary Purge, 1946.

Registration of securities

A second measure introduced simultaneously with the monetary purge was the suspension of all market transactions in securities and the prescription of official registration for all domestically and foreign held bonds and shares of Netherlands origin, and Treasury paper as well as foreign securities held by Dutch nationals, in order to verify and establish legal and uncontaminated ownership. All securities that did not meet this test could be expropriated, following due process of law. This measure supplemented and supported the action in the monetary field and was of invaluable assistance in firming up the tax base.

Fiscal measures

A third set of measures was taken in the fiscal field. Despite the severe austerity applied to ordinary budget expenditures, the costs involved in the reconstruction of the economic infrastructure of the country, war-damage compensation to corporate and private victims, the rebuilding of a national defense system, large-scale lending to the Netherlands East Indies and other overseas parts of the Kingdom to assist in their rehabilitation, and the subsidisation of prices of essential goods in order to keep the cost of living down, required government spending going considerably beyond the revenue from current taxes at the greatly depressed national income level.

Since during the war years tax evasion had been practiced on a large scale and tax assessment had run into a backlog, supplementary tax declarations were imposed with respect to all existing direct taxes, and provisional tax assessments were made covering the year 1944 and the first eight months of 1945. In order to speed up the collection of tax arrears and in anticipation of the announced reconstruction taxes, a system of voluntary and obligatory tax deposits (advance payments to the Treasury) was introduced which by the end of 1946 amounted to over 1,800 million guilders.

To supplement the revenue from normal taxes, two special reconstruction taxes were imposed:

(1) a so-called capital increase levy on the accrual during the war years of all personal wealth (money holdings and all other assets taxable under the existing wealth tax), at a rate of 50 to 90 per cent differentiated on the basis of a propriety test of the nature of the acquisition and the amount of the increase;

(2) a so-called once-for-all capital levy on all personal wealth at the end of the war, at a rate of 4 to 20 per cent by application of a progression scale.

The collection of these special taxes, the total yield of which amounted to over 3,000 million guilders, was spread over a number of years, and to the extent that they were not paid out of blocked accounts these levies contributed considerably to counteracting otherwise generated new inflationary pressures.

With a view to making the Government budget a better policy instrument adjusted to the circumstances, its structure was for the time being modified. Instead of the traditional division in two parts, a current account and a capital account, the current budget was divided in an ordinary account, an extra-ordinary account and a separate budget chapter for the newly established Agricultural Equalization Fund. The ordinary account covered normal recurrent expenditures. The extra-ordinary account covered all expenditures that were directly connected with those functions of the Government that were undertaken to cope with the dislocation of the economy, including war damages, and, therefore, were considered to be of a temporary character (the administration and liquidation of the war heritage). The budget of the Agricultural Equalization Fund served to give an estimate of the balance of the cost of farm and consumer subsidies and the yield of agricultural export levies, the former being required to ensure a reasonable remuneration to the farmers while at the same time keeping the food bill of the consumers down. Its actual outcome was highly dependent on changes in world market prices; and given the objectives just mentioned, the balance of this account could not be predicted reliably. The capital budget maintained its traditional character of covering expenditures that increased the durable assets of the public domain and the revenues derived from those assets. Particularly the introduction of the extra-ordinary account in the current budget proved to serve an extremely useful purpose because it avoided the mixing up of recurrent and non-recurrent expenditures, facilitated a special surveillance and an appropriate phasing of the latter, and embodied a constant reminder that those expendititures were temporary and should be abolished as soon as possible. Budget figures are given in Table II.

Internal controls

A fourth set of measures consisted of internal controls on private consumption, private investment, prices, interest rates and wages. A system of rationing of all major consumption goods was already in force and was continued for economic and social reasons longer than in any other Western European country. All private investments were subject to licensing, and even priority investments were approved only to the extent that construction materials and equipment goods could be procured domestically or foreign exchange could be made available for their procurement abroad. Strictly enforced price controls were maintained on all important commodities, services and rents. The rate of interest for long-term public borrowing was held down at 3 per cent. Wage rates were established for the country as a whole in consultation with the Labor Foundation composed of representatives of organized labor,

Table II *Central Government Revenues and Expenditures, 1946–1952* (in millions of guilders)

	1946	1947	1948	1949	1950	1951	1952
A. Current Revenues							
Ordinary	3.595	3,977	3,849	4,658	4,647	5,357	5,546
Special levies	—	99	2,049	564	96	81	86
Counterpart funds[1]	—	—	240	305	279	203	827
Total	3,595	4,076	6,140	5,527	5,022	5,461	6,459
B. Current Expenditures							
Ordinary[2]	2,205	2,225	2,733	2,827	2,897	3,357	3,720
Extra-ordinary	1,554	1,763	1,415	981	856	771	587
Agricultural Equalization Fund	424	494	468	266	223	143	67
Total	4,183	4,482	4,616	4,074	3,976	4,271	4,374
C. Current Balance	- 588	- 406	1,524	1,453	1,046	1,370	2,085
D. Capital Revenues	108	95	208	140	436	301	275
E. Capital Expenditures	407	642	546	391	982	1,296	1,214
F. Capital Balance	- 299	- 547	- 338	- 251	- 546	- 995	- 939

G. Total Revenues	3,703	4,171	6,348	5,667	5,458	5,942	6,734
H. Total Expenditures	4,590	5,124	5,162	4,464	4,958	5,567	5,588
I. Overall Balance	− 887	− 953	1,186	1,203	500	375	1,146
J. Total Expenditures as percentage of National Income	46.68	42.45	36.27	27.97	27.95	28.46	27.71

[1] Mostly used for redemption of National Debt.
[2] Inclusive of redemption of National Debt.

Source: Budget Messages, Ministry of Finance, 1953–1955.

employers' organizations and the Government. They were kept below the pre-war level in real terms and their increase from year to year was so moderate that they hardly kept pace with the rise in the cost of living (see Table IV). At the same time, wages in agriculture and other low-wage sectors were adjusted upward to the general level for reasons of social equity. These wage policies were particularly successful and were an important factor in preventing an inflationary spiral at a critical time. Although over the three-year period 1946–1949 wholesale prices increased by an average of $7\frac{1}{2}$ per cent per annum, the cost of living rose by less than 4 per cent per annum, the difference mainly to be explained by effective rent and wage controls.

Measures with respect to foreign trade and payments

The four sets of measures discussed so far were aimed at and contributed greatly to containing total effective demand. Other measures were taken simultaneously with the purpose of rapidly increasing domestic production and supplying the country from abroad with the variety of goods needed for its economic recovery. Adequate imports were a conditio sine qua non for restoring productivity, providing the people with food, clothing, fuel and shelter, starting to rebuild what had been devastated (high priority was given te reconstruction of the infrastructure) and supplying the economy with equipment goods and raw materials for the all-important processing industries. Since exports and income from invisibles had fallen to a negligible level and could only increase with the rehabilitation of productive capacity, a considerable deficit in the balance of payments on current account had to be accepted for some time. These deficits amounted to the equivalent of US$ 500 million in 1946, US$ 625 million in 1947 and US$ 425 million in 1948.[1]

[1]) Before September 19, 1949: 2.66 Netherlands guilders = 1 US dollar.

The deficits were financed by:

(1) further drawing down of the gold stock;

(2) liquidating foreign assets, including foreign securities;

(3) foreign loans;

(4) Marshall aid, but this did not become available until the second half of 1948 when, for lack of foreign means of payments (especially dollars) the recovery effort was on the brink of collapsing.

In order to secure a rational allocation of the scarce resources, all exports, imports and foreign payments were subject to licensing and an obligation to surrender all foreign exchange receipts was imposed.

As a consequence of the international supply conditions prevailing in the first post-war years, a much higher percentage of total imports had to be obtained from the Western Hemisphere than had been the case in the pre-war period. Thus the import surpluses in 1946, 1947 and 1948 were due respectively to trade with the United States, Canada and a few other American countries, in the amount of 58.1, 67.9 and 59.5 per cent of the total, as compared with 20.6 per cent in 1938. Consequently, most of the extraordinary funds that were mobilized were spent in the Western Hemisphere. With the more important European trading partners trade and payments were regulated by means of bilateral agreements through which it was possible to maintain a reasonable payments equilibrium in the European sphere.

The economic performance from 1946 until the beginning of Marshall Aid

Owing to the rapid re-equipment of industry and agriculture with capital goods and raw materials, the reabsorbation of the labor force into the country's productive potential, and (last, but not least) the restauration of public services and transportation, real GNP increased between 1946 and 1948 by almost 20 per cent per annum. Industrial production surpassed the pre-war level in 1947 and the productivity of agriculture, despite a serious setback caused by the unusually cold winter and dry summer of 1947, was practically restored in 1948. As overall domestic consumption increased at a lower rate than GNP, a margin for rapidly rising exports was created: from the equivalent of only $300 million in 1946, exports rose to over $700 million in 1947 and to $1,000 million in 1948. Shipping and other services started also to contribute again to the country's foreign exchange earnings. At the same time, imports continued to grow, doubling between 1946 and 1948, and the succession of large current account deficits augmented by sizeable transfers to the overseas parts of the Kingdom rapidly exhausted the country's reserves (mainly official gold holding and private foreign assets) and its possibilities to obtain foreign credits. For balance of payments figures reference is made to Table III.

Although in 1948 a marked improvement began to develop in the current account relationship with the non-dollar area (mainly through the services account), even resulting in a modest surplus, this did not help much to alleviate the acute dollar shortage which The Netherlands, like other European countries, faced. The United States remained the principal supplier, exports to that country were difficult to expand and even surpluses earned elsewhere were of limited use because net earnings in other currencies could not be converted into dollars. This set of conditions constituted the most serious bottleneck to further progress. Fortunately, it was overcome when, in the later part of 1948, the European Recovery Program (the so-called Marshall Plan) came into operation, enabling the reconstruction of Western Europe to be carried on and even to be accelerated, thereby contributing considerably to the stabilisation efforts.

The internal situation was characterised, despite the elimination of the large money-overhang and the rapid improvement in the economic performance, by an early return of inflationary pressures. Under the impact of the monetary purge, the money supply had been reduced from 10,900 million guilders in May 1945, to 4,100 million guilders at the end of that year. Thereafter it rose steadily until it was practically stabilised at a level of around 7,200 million guilders in May 1948. Expressed as a percentage of national income, the volume of free money increased rather substantially in the course of 1946, remained at that level during 1947 and dropped again to the end of 1945 ratio in 1948 (see Table I).

There is no doubt that the financial operations of the Government were largely responsible for these developments. After providing the economy with an adequate money supply, direct releases from blocked accounts and the expansion of bank credit to the private sector were kept to modest amounts. During this three year period, however, extra-ordinary current (reconstruction) expenditures reached their highest volume, causing considerable budgetary deficits (on a cash basis); and it was only in the final year that the offsetting effect of the collection of the special levies, the adoption and assessment of which had suffered parliamentary and administrative delays, brought considerable relief. The high yield of these extra-ordinary taxes resulted in 1948 in a large overall surplus (see Table II). It should be mentioned, however, that the deficits in 1946 and 1947 were not entirely financed by recourse to the banking system; to a certain extent they were financed without creating money, for example by borrowing domestically from non-banks or were related to spending outside of the country. On the other hand, insofar as tax payments were received from blocked accounts or tax deposits made in earlier years, and were spent by the Government, of course in free money, this had the same monetary effect as deficit financing. This happened in 1948 to such a degree that despite the large overall surplus on Government

Table III *Balance of Payments* (in millions of guilders)

	1946	1947	1948	1949	1950	1951	1952
A. Goods and services							
Exports f.o.b.	816	1,905	2,666	3,673	5,204	7,023	7,684
Imports f.o.b.	−2,146	−3,759	−4,289	−4,733	−6,937	−8,069	−7,168
Trade balance	−1,330	−1,854	−1,623	−1,060	−1,733	−1,046	516
Transportation, investment income and other services (net)	18	187	487	838	667	956	1,254
Total	−1,312	−1,667	−1,136	− 222	−1,066	− 90	1,370
B. Private donations and capital movements	− 37	170	127	− 41	49	90	91
C. Miscellaneous official financing	− 47	− 242	− 91	− 206	− 327	− 174	− 242
D. Net errors and omissions	− 48	—	—	− 32	− 15	− 150	− 7
E. Net financing of overseas parts of the Kingdom	− 193	− 296	− 369	− 481	− 3	− 122	− 91
F. Surplus or deficit (−) (A through E)	−1,637	−2,035	−1,469	− 982	−1,362	− 446	1,621

G. Compulsory sale of private assets	306	747	432	205	134	130	93
H. ECA/MSA grants and credits (net)[1]	—	—	615	720	814	503	229
I. OEEC drawing rights (net) and EPU initial credit position[2]	—	—	39	141	328	—	—
J. Long term credits	704	701	418	3	163	—	66
K. Monetary gold (increase-)	– 22	563	153	– 86	– 305	– 10	– 875
L. Monetary movements (excluding K)	649	24	– 188	– 1	228	– 177	– 1,121
	– 1,637	2,035	1,469	982	1,362	446	– 1,129

[1] So-called direct Marshal Aid.

[2] OEEC drawing rights were mutual credit facilities among OEEC members; when the EPU (European Payments Union) was created a limited number of countries, among them the Netherlands, were given extra credit facilities above their quota, a so-called initial credit balance, and some others an initial debit balance.

Sources: IMF Balance of Payments Yearbook, 1946-1952.
Annual Reports, Netherlands Bank, 1946-1954.

Table IV *Prices and Wages, 1945-1952*[1]
(1938 = 100)

	1945[2]	1946	1947	1948	1949	1950	1951	1952
Wholesale prices	217	247	267	278	289	325	400	394
Cost of living	178	190	198	204	216	237	261	259
Wage rates (industry & agriculture)	161	173	179	186	193	207	223	225
Real wages	90	91	90	91	89	87	85	87

[1] December

[2] 1937-1938 = 100.

Source: Central Bureau of Statistics, The Hague.

account there still continued to be substantial inflationary financing by the Treasury in the amount of 572 million guilders. Nevertheless, in the course of that year the increase in the money supply started to decelerate while GNP continued to rise at a rapid pace. This soon brought about a much desired improvement in the over-liquidity of the economy.

Although the developments in the money supply had been temporarily less satisfactory, inflationary tendencies remained suppressed by the maintenance of rationing, licensing, subsidies and price controls, and very effective policies of wage restraint, as mentioned earlier. The performance of prices and wages is illustrated in Table IV.

In appraising these figures it should be noted that wholesale prices reflected largely the growing impact and the rising trend of import prices. Export prices rose considerably less and the terms of trade deteriorated from 113 in 1946 (1938 = 100) to 96 in 1948. The modest rise in the cost of living is mainly explained by the import component, and wage rates rather followed than led.

Marshall Aid

In the final quarter of 1948, Marshall Aid started to flow in. Over the five-year period 1948-1952 the Netherlands benefited from this source in a total amount of $968.8 million, of which 84 per cent in grants and 16 per cent in loans, all to be spent in the United States. The introduction of the Marshall Plan at the same time decisively stimulated intra-European cooperation, particularly in the field of trade and payments. It was instrumental in the creation of the Organisation for European Economic Cooperation (OEEC) and the European Payments Union (EPU), which led the way toward intra-European trade liberalisation and multilateral credit arrangements. Net drawings by the Netherlands under the latter scheme amounted during the years 1948-1950 to $156 million equivalent. (For the distribution of these inflows over the years, compare Table III, H and I.)

The availability of these sources of aid enabled the country to carry on its reconstruction effort supported by large foreign imports, particularly of raw materials and equipment goods, which greatly helped to meet rising demand especially for investment and exports, out of domestic production. One of the results was that the temporary interference of the Government with the economy could be reduced, which meant at the same time a considerable saving on public (extra-ordinary) current expenditures.

In the monetary field, advantage was taken of Marshall Aid by using most of the guilder counterpart funds of the grants received, directly or indirectly (via the budget), for redemption of Government debt with the central bank – which meant their sterilisation. During the period 1948-1952, 2.3 billion guilders were extracted from circulation in this manner. This compensated to a large extent the monetary expansion resulting from Treasury financing, which amounted over the same period to about 500 million guilders, and from money creation by the banking system in transactions with the private sector. Consequently, by the end of 1948 the overall money supply began to stabilise (see Table I).[1]

[1] For a detailed discussion of the importance of the Marshall Plan for The Netherlands and European cooperation, reference is made to 'Road to Recovery', a publication of the Ministry of Foreign Affairs, The Hague, 1954.

THE PERIOD OF NEAR-EQUILIBRIUM AND PRICE LIBERALISATION, 1949

Internal and external performance

Developments in 1949 were most encouraging. Although a certain amount of repressed inflation was still present, no new inflationary pressures were being added. In fact, from the middle of 1948 until the middle of 1950, a practically stable money supply went hand in hand with a further substantial increase of national income (at market prices), which rose from 14.2 billion guilders in 1948 to 17.7 billion guilders in 1950. The ratio of money to national income dropped further, by 10 percentage points, in that period (see Table I).

Whereas in 1948 the massive yield of the special levies – partly paid out of blocked accounts and tax deposits – had been the major cause of the overall budgetary surplus, the almost equal surplus achieved in 1949 resulted from a considerable increase of ordinary revenues, the beginning of a phasing out of the extra-ordinary (reconstruction) expeditures and a marked reduction of the deficit of the Agricultural Equalization Fund. This greatly reduced the money creation by the Government, to an insignificant 116 million guilders.

The conjunction of rapidly increasing national output, higher imports and a stable money supply enabled the Government in the course of 1949 to start a cautious dismantling of the comprehensive system of internal controls which the scarcity situation had necessitated. Rationing was almost completely abolished, price controls were relaxed and food subsidies strongly curtailed, but wages and housing rents remained strictly controlled. Wholesale prices continued to be influenced by rising prices in foreign markets, and the cost of living index rose by 6 per cent reflecting the reduction in food subsidies and the 5 per cent general wage increase that was granted in 1948 (see Table IV).

The restauration of the economy, supported by Marshall Aid and the concomitant intensification of trade and payments relations with other Western European countries, did not fail to have a favorable impact on the balance of payments position. Exports increased considerably. In 1948 the value of exports had risen 45 per cent over the preceding year; in 1949 the increase was 51 per cent. As imports increased less rapidly, the percentage of imports covered by exports rose from 44 in 1947 to 60 in 1948 and to 72 in 1949, approaching the pre-war relationship. This favorable development in the foreign trade sector, together with a remarkable increase in the surplus on services account caused the deficit on the current account of the balance of payments to drop from roughtly $625 million equivalent in 1947 to $425 million equivalent in 1948 and to $89 million equivalent in 1949 (at the rate of 2.66 guilders = 1 U.S. dollar).

Equilibrium still on fragile foundations

Three factors, however, caused the equilibrium that was achieved by the end of 1949 still to be incomplete and not too firmly established. They were:

(1) the large amount of secondary liquidity in the financial system;

(2) the large volume of pent-up demand that could be expected to take advantage of the liberalisation of consumption and imports;

(3) the impact of the international exchange rate adjustments that took place in September 1949.

Although money holdings at the end of 1949 were down to 47 per cent of national income, near-money (mostly time and saving deposits) and short term government debt held by the public totaled over 3 billion guilders, equal to roughly 20 per cent of national income. These near-money holdings were far in excess of desired secondary liquidity and could readily be converted into money or used for tax payments. Moreover, there was still a residual of blocked money in the amount of 460 million guilders tied to certain options, among which the special fiscal facilities mentioned earlier. There were no more quantitative credit controls, and with the high liquidity of the commercial banks the elasticity of the credit system constituted an additional potential threat to monetary stability.

Demands of all kinds had been suppressed for almost 10 years and became increasingly hungry for satisfaction. This applied as well to consumption goods as to investment goods for replacement and expansion, and there was a strong desire to build up inventories and raw material stocks. With the opening of the European markets, new possibilities presented themselves for intra-European trade on a much larger scale than was possible between the European countries and the United States; even with the Marshall Aid, imports from the United States continued to be limited by the scarcity of the dollar (and the inconvertibility of the European currencies into dollars).

In September 1949 the British pound was devalued by 30.5 per cent in relation to the U.S. dollar, and a number of other currencies in and outside of Europe wholly or partly followed that course. Among those going almost as far as sterling was the Netherlands guilder, which devalued by 30.2 per cent, to a rate of 3.80 guilders = 1 U.S. dollar. The Netherlands Government took this decision in order to avoid a fundamental disequilibrium under the new circumstances, to maintain its competitive position vis-à-vis the United Kingdom and other European countries that were significant to the Dutch position and to improve the competitive position in Western Hemisphere markets. The Marshall Aid gave only temporary relief with respect to the dollar problem. The overall balance of payments was still in considerable deficit, mainly owing to rather substantial amortization payments on foreign debt and net financing of Indonesia and other overseas parts of the Kingdom, and the foreign exchange reserves (gold and foreign exchange holdings plus the net balance outstanding on payments agreement accounts, including EPU) amounted to only $278 million at the end of 1949, which was completely insufficient to meet a temporary setback for a country so dependent on imports. An additional consideration which guided the authorities in not following some other European countries that devalued less was the fact that there was still a residuum of domestic subsidies and price controls, and prudence dictated leaving a margin for cost and price increases resulting from further internal liberalisation measures.

The devaluation of the guilder had the unavoidable effect of raising the prices in terms of guilders of imports from those countries that had not devalued or had devalued less, and this did not fail to have a considerable impact on domestic prices and some effect on export prices (the import content of the country's exports being at that time about 30 per cent). As a result of the exchange rate adjustments, the Netherlands economy was also faced with a significant change in international competitive conditions, and the impact thereof made itself felt almost simultaneously with the liberalisation of European trade as from January 1, 1950. The most important developments were a significant shift of imports from the dollar to the sterling area and a rapid increase of trade with the OECD countries, especially Belgium and Germany.

The three factors mentioned in this section contributed to the activation of the inflationary potential that still existed and this brought the economy into a new phase characterised by intensive demand and a revival of inflationary pressures.

REVIVAL OF INFLATIONARY PRESSURES AND DEFLATIONARY MEASURES, 1950 TO MID-1951

Intensification of demand and the absorption of liquidity

At the beginning of 1950 the stage was set for a strong intensification of effective demand, in particular for foreign raw materials and finished goods. In conformity with the real income conditions of the larger part of the population, real consumption hardly increased. Strong demand pressures, however, developed with respect to investment goods and for the purposes of replenishing stocks and providing for better assorted inventories. The rise in prices triggered off by the devaluation became more pronounced when the Korean War broke out, which caused a heavy wave of speculative buying in anticipation of world price increases and scarcities. In fact, the second half of 1950 and the first quarter of 1951 was a period of worldwide inflation. The Netherlands economy has always been highly sensitive to international price movements, the ratio between the value of imports and exports of goods and services to total national income being higher than in any other industrialised country (at that time the ratio was more than 50 per cent), and the domestic price level was strongly affected by these new developments.

During the 12 months of 1950 wholesale prices rose by 12 per cent and the cost of living by about 8 per cent. These price increases became even more pronounced in the first half of 1951 when wholesale prices rose by 11 per cent and the cost of living by about

8 per cent. Moreover, the rising prices of imports were not sufficiently compensated by the rise of export prices, which brought about a considerable deterioration in the terms of trade. Consequently, the percentage of imports covered by exports dropped from 72 in 1949 to 68 in 1950 and to 66 in the first half of 1951. Owing to a high rate of earnings on the services account and a continued inflow of capital, the overall balance of payments remained in surplus in 1950, but in the first half of 1951, when Marshall Aid started to taper off and the existing credit facilities under the European Payments Union became exhausted, a payments deficit appeared and the official gold and net foreign exchange reserves began to decline alarmingly (from $400 million at the end of 1950 to $280 million at the end of June 1951).

Monetary developments in this period showed clearly that the buying waves were financed by the use of liquid assets (money and secondary liquidity) carried over from previous years and by an expansion of bank credit. During 1950 total liquid assets declined by 940 million guilders and net credit expansion by the commercial banks amounted to 370 million guilders, making a total of 1,310 million guilders. Net sales of foreign exchange by the banking system amounted to 1,100 million guilders, the difference to be explained by a deflationary effect of the Government's budgetary transactions amounting to about 210 million guilders.

The first half of 1951 showed a somewhat similar outcome, with a reduction of liquid assets of 530 million guilders and an expansion of commercial bank credit by 230 million guilders, making a total of 760 million guilders that was more than absorbed by net sales of foreign exchange amounting to 830 million guilders. Now the public sector ran a small deficit, but this was not caused by the Government's budget, which remained in surplus, but by the financial operations of the local authorities. Simultaneously, national income increased at a rapid rate both in real terms and, as a result of a rise in prices, even more in nominal terms, implying a rise in the transaction needs for liquid balances. The ultimate result was that, despite a release of practically the entire remaining amount of blocked money in 1950, total liquid assets were equal to 49 per cent of national income at the end of June 1951, as against 67 per cent at the end of 1949. This sharp reduction of the liquidity of the economy laid a much firmer foundation for the final establishment of internal and external equilibrium than had existed before.

Resumption of deliberate deflationary policies

During 1950 it was deemed feasible to allow the forces which pressed on the internal position to operate as freely as possible. Corrective measures were not taken apart from issuing consolidation loans and increasing the discount rate from 2.5 to 3 per cent, a change which was actually no more than a signal because the rate remained ineffective, given the high liquidity of the banks. The Treasury, faced with the need to repay large amounts of short-term debt to the public and the banks, could meet these requirements by drawing on considerable non-budgetary resources (mostly releases from counterpart funds and revenue from gold sold to the central bank) and on its own balances with the central bank. However, from the beginning of 1951 a more vigorous monetary, fiscal and incomes policy was adopted.

On January 1, 1951 rather stringent credit controls were imposed on the commercial banks. These controls required the banks to hold certain amounts of liquid assets against their deposits and included short term Government debt in the definition of bank liquidity, thus practically freezing the bulk of the banks' holdings of Government debt. About the middle of April the official discount rate was increased to 4 per cent. One month later, owing to a continued weakening of the foreign exchange position, the requirement of a 25 per cent advance deposit on purchases of forward exchange was introduced. This reinforced the effect of the credit restrictions. As the demand for commercial credit remained strong, excess bank liquidity was soon exhausted and in the late spring many banks had to turn to the credit facilities of the central bank, and so the official discount rate became effective.

In the middle of March 1951 the Government adopted a disinflationary program which included:

(1) a reduction of the remaining food subsidies and other reductions of current Government expenditures (although defense expenditures were increased);

(2) prompter collection of direct taxes;

(3) increased rates for some indirect taxes (e.g., turnover tax) and direct taxes (e.g., company profit tax);

(4) the issue of a long-term loan in the domestic market;

(5) sharper direct controls on investments, in particular of municipalities;

(6) reduction of the building program.

These actions found support in a tripartite agreement, concluded in March between Government, organized management and labor, to limit the compensating rise in wage rates (compensating for the cost of living increase) to 5 per cent, which implied a decrease of real wages by 5 per cent from the level of September 1949.

The introduction of this comprehensive set of disinflationary measures did not fail to have a marked impact on the economy; the more so as it coincided with the end of the Korean War boom, which manifested itself in a rapid decline of import demand, mostly for raw materials, in most of the industrialized countries and a sharp reduction in many raw material prices. In The Netherlands, as elsewhere, the expectations of the business community, which had been bullish during 1950 and the first quarter of 1951, began to change. Applications for new import licenses had begun to taper off already in the second quarter. At the same time consumer demand fell sharply, and from the middle of 1951 public investment slowed down and stocks were rapidly reduced.

THE ESTABLISHMENT OF INTERNAL AND EXTERNAL EQUILIBRIUM, MID-1951 TO MID-1952

During the second half of 1951 the overall balance of payments returned to surplus by means of a remarkable improvement in the balance of trade. The deficit suffered in the first half of the year could be largely replenished; and between June 1951 and June 1952 the net official reserve position improved by $500 million, reaching a level of about $800 million. The percentage of imports that was covered by exports increased in the second half of 1951 to 77; in 1952 it became as high as 94 per cent. Underlying these changes in the external position were the effects of the disinflationary measures taken in the earlier months of 1951, combined with favorable developments in international markets (the terms of trade improved for the first time in many years) and the fact that consumers and enterprises had exhausted the liquid funds accumulated during the period of repressed inflation. Credit expansion in the private sector slowed down to what could be considered commensurate with the growth of the economy. The Central Government's budgetary transactions had a deflationary effect that largely offset the short-term borrowing of the municipalities from the banking system.

Both wholesale prices and the index of the cost of living stopped rising and even showed a tendency to decline. Money wages increased marginally and real wages a little more. One of the most remarkable outcomes of the entire seven-year period was that the level of real wages was still about the same at the end as it was at the beginning, but social provisions had greatly improved and no serious unemployment had developed despite a reduction of personnel in the Central Government civil service (exclusive of military departments) from roughly 125,000 in 1945 to 75,000 in 1952.

So, in mid-1952 the country had a healthy economy. The domestic price level was stabilised, budget equilibrium was well established, the balance of payments and the foreign reserve positions were strong. Confidence in the guilder was fully restored. The reconstruction and stabilisation efforts had succeeded. The sacrifices made by the Dutch people during a long period of austerity had not been in vain.

But what was the financial burden in terms of Government debt and debt service obligations that had to be carried forward?

GOVERNMENT DEBT AND DEBT MANAGEMENT

Internal debt

During the war years, as a direct and indirect result of the occupation, a huge financial deficit on Government account had accumulated. This had been financed to a relatively small extent by long-term borrowing (via the issue of semi-obligatory war loans) but mainly by the placement of Treasury paper with the banking system. When at the end of 1945 the amount of the Central Government's domestic debt was assessed it was put at 22.4 billion guilders, against 3.7 billion guilders at the end of 1938. The consolidated debt had increased from 3.2 billion guilders to 5.8 billion guilders, the floating debt (net) from 0.5 billion guilders to 16.1 billion guilders. In this latter figure were included, apart from Treasury paper in circulation and with the central bank, other short-term obligations – mostly deposits of institutional investors in anticipation of subscriptions to consolidation loans to be issued (so-called pre-subscription accounts) and credit balances on current account of public and semi-public institutions held with the Treasury – as well as estimated unpaid claims on the Government on account of war damages (see Table V).

In the course of the next few years this initial assessment of the internal Government debt underwent two major upward adjustments.

The first adjustment resulted from the agreement between the Government and the Netherlands Bank of February 26, 1947 under which the Government, for the purpose of cleaning up the balance sheet of the central bank, took over from the Netherlands Bank an amount of 5,933 million (worthless) Reichsmarks accumulated under the occupation against a compensation of 4,471 million guilders. Of this amount, 1,500 million guilders was accounted for by a book entry, 'Government debt to the Netherlands Bank'; 2,100 million guilders was paid to the Bank in Treasury bills and the remaining amount was settled in cash or other instruments.

The second adjustment took place in 1949 after the coming into effect of the Law on Material War Damages, the indemnity provisions of which were more liberal than those of the immediate post-war Royal Decree that was basic to the original estimate. The item 'claims on account of war damages' was raised accordingly in the Government debt account as at December 31, 1949 by 1,200 million guilders minus the amount paid out during the year 1949 (400 million guilders) for indemnification.

Taking these adjustments into account, the total domestic debt (net) declined during the period from the end of December 1945 to the end of June 1952 from 27.6 billion guilders to 19.3 billion guilders. This decline resulted from actual war-damage indemnity payments (3.3 billion guilders); the use of counterpart funds of Marshall Aid, partly via the budget, partly directly for debt redemption (2.3 billion guilders): contractual amortization of long-term loans; payment of taxes by means of Treasury paper; and, for the remainder, from cash settlement of maturing short-term debt.

Also, the structure of the internal debt improved considerably. Excluding the book debt to the Netherlands Bank (agreement of 2-26-1947) the repayment of which was subject to special provisions of a monetary policy character, and the claims on the Government on account of war damages the realization of which was under budgetary control, the amount of the floating debt (net) declined between the end of 1945 and June 1952 from 11.1 billion

Table V *Debt of the Central Government* (in billions of guilders)

End of	1938	1945	1946	1947	1948	1949	1950	1951	June 1952
Domestic Debt (gross)									
Consolidated	3.2	5.8	7.2	7.1	7.2	7.7	8.4	8.8	8.6
Debt to Netherlands Bank (agreement of 2-26-1947)				1.5	1.5	1.5	1.5	1.5	1.3
Floating									
Treasury paper		8.8	6.0	9.1	8.6	8.5	7.0	5.9	5.7
Other short-term obligations		2.6	3.7	3.7	2.8	2.3	1.7	2.1	2.1
Claims on acc. of war damages		5.0	4.5	3.8	3.3	4.1	3.5	3.1	2.9
Total Floating	0.5[1]	16.4	14.2	16.6	14.7	14.9	12.2	11.1	10.7
Total Domestic Debt	3.7[1]	22.2	21.4	25.2	23.4	24.1	22.1	21.4	20.5
Foreign Debt (gross)									
Consolidated	—	0.5	1.0	1.0	1.9	2.9	3.1	3.0	3.0
Floating	—	0.5	0.3	1.0	0.4	0.5	0.3	0.2	0.1
Total Foreign Debt	—	1.0	1.3	2.0	2.3	3.4	3.4	3.2	3.1

Total Government Debt (gross)		23.2	22.7	27.2	25.7	25.5	25.5	24.6	23.6
Assets of the Treasury[2]		0.3	1.7	0.7	0.8	1.3	1.1	0.8	1.2
Total Government Debt (net)	3.7	22.9	21.0	26.5	24.9	26.2	24.4	23.8	22.4

[1] Net.

[2] Predominantly, domestic.

Sources: Annex 13 to Budget Message, 1953.
Annual Report, Netherlands Bank, 1953.

guilders (after adjustment 13.2) to 6.6 billion guilders. The consolidated debt increased over the same period from 5.8 billion guilders to 8.6 billion guilders. Government bond issues, net of conversions, absorbed 5.2 billion guilders, of which 2.7 from blocked accounts and 2.5 from new savings (mostly institutional) involving to a large extent consolidation of floating debt on presubscription accounts. Particularly during 1951, the offering of long-term loans was used as a policy instrument for the purpose of reducing both primary and secondary liquidity as a disinflationary measure.

In order to keep the burden of the public debt service down and for reasons of distributional equity, the instruments of debt which the Government issued were of a low interest bearing type and, except for Treasury bills and notes, generally with long maturities. The main instrument for the absorption of blocked money offered in 1946 and subscribed to in an amount of 1.8 billion guilders consisted of a 3 per cent 50-year loan. In 1947 subscription was opened to a loan for the conversion of the still outstanding parts of a number of war loans (and one pre-war loan) bearing interest rates of 4 or 3½ per cent and 20 years maturity. This conversion loan, which was semi-obligatory amounted to 2.7 billion guilders, carried 3 per cent interest the first 10 years and 3½ per cent thereafter, and had a maturity of 40 years. Subsequent loans issued in 1948, 1949 and 1950 were mostly placed with social security funds and institutional investors; they had either a shorter maturity than the 1947 conversion loan or carried a somewhat higher interest rate (3¼ per cent). In 1951 a number of Government issues were placed, partly for the consolidation of outstanding Treasury paper, partly for the purpose of absorbing fresh money. In that year the long-term interest rate on newly issued Government bonds rose first to 3½ and then to 4 per cent, reflecting the tightening of the capital market. In 1952 the Government abstained from borrowing, but the 4 per cent interest rate was maintained as a maximum for long-term borrowing by the lower public authorities.

External debt

By the end of 1945 official foreign debt in the amount of 1 billion guilders had been incurred, mostly for services and supplies received from allied Governments during and immediately after liberation. During the whole period under discussion, the end-of-year foreign debt figure did not increase beyond 3.4 billion guilders, which was reached at the end of 1949. In fact, more than one third of the increase (0.9 billion guilders out of 2.4 billion) resulted from the devaluation of the guilder in terms of creditors' currencies.

In the years preceding Marshall Aid, deficits on the balance of payments were covered for almost two thirds by the proceeds of sales of Netherlands assets abroad and by utilizing part of the available gold and foreign exchange reserves, and for roughly one third by net borrowing (see Table II). The main sources of credit during this period were the U.S. Export-Import-Bank and the International Bank for Reconstruction and Development (each for about $200 million). Drawings on the International Monetary Fund amounted to some $75 million equivalent, Belgium extended help ful credits on a smaller scale and some use was also made of credit margins available under bilateral payments arrangements.

As was mentioned earlier, Marshall Aid started flowing in as from the final quarter of 1948 and was received to a large extent in the form of grants; the loan portion amounted to about 540 million guilders. An almost equal amount of credit was obtained by net use of OEEC drawing rights and the EPU initial credit position. New loans in relatively modest amounts were raised in 1950 in Belgium and Switzerland. The liquidation of assets abroad continued but yielded declining proceeds. At the same time, important redemptions took place on various loans, particularly those with short maturities, and by the end of June 1952 total foreign debt stood at 3.1 billion guilders, all of which was consolidated except for 100 million guilders. If all Marshall Aid had been made available on a loan basis, the Netherlands foreign indebtedness would have been just twice as high.

Debt service burden

The servicing of the total Government debt (internal and external) outstanding at the end of June 1952 required in that year 866 million guilders, representing 4.2 per cent of national income and almost 16 per cent of total Government expenditures. These percentages were bound to decline with the future increase of the national income and the amount of budget expenditures, as they actually did.

Scheduled payments on the outstanding foreign debt, mostly carrying low interest rates, totaled the equivalent of $82 million in 1952, $65 million in 1953 and $46 million in 1954; from then on they would remain at about that level until 1966. This meant a foreign debt service burden in 1952 of about 3 per cent of total foreign exchange earnings on current account, dropping rapidly in the following years.

SUMMARY AND CONCLUSION

During the first three and a half years after liberation The Netherlands, the longest enemy-occupied and most heavily war-damaged country in Western Europe, had to struggle ahead on its own, except for one short-term loan from the U.S. Export-Import Bank (with a negative security pledge clause attached), one long-term reconstruction loan from the World Bank, a modest drawing on the IMF and some miscellaneous credits. Unlike former enemy countries Germany and Japan, the country did not benefit from large U.S. dollar spending for post-war military and civil purposes. Intra-European commercial relations were severely hampered by quantitative trade and payments restrictions, and bilateral credit margins allowed by these countries were rather insignificant. At the same time, The Netherlands could not avoid assuming the burden of considerable net financing of overseas parts of the Kingdom, especially the East Indies (future Indonesia), where the modern sector of the economy had heavily suffered from the Japanese occupation.

The Netherlands, therefore, had to put its house in order largely on its own strength, stabilize and restore its battered and money-flooded economy with all the energy the people could muster and all the resources it could mobilize, including its remaining official reserves and private assets abroad. The monetary purge drained off the dangerous overhang of excessive internal liquidity created during the war and brought the effective money supply under Government control. Given the strong pressure of unsatisfied needs, strict demand management, rationing and price control had to be exercised in order to suppress inflation.

Direct consumption, investment and import controls and drastic monetary, fiscal and debt management policies, together with a comprehensive incomes policy (not restricted to wages), were applied to achieve this objective. Nevertheless, in the first few years the large public expenditures that were required to reconstruct the economy and keep the cost of living down could not be covered by current ordinary tax revenues, even when supplemented by payments of tax arrears. The financing of the Government deficit by drawing down the large cash reserves that had resulted from bond issues to absorb blocked money and from tax deposits did not fail to have an inflationary impact. But this subsided in 1948 when the Treasury began to benefit from the yield of the special levies which, insofar as these were paid in free money (and not from blocked accounts), reduced the expansionary monetary effect of the financial operations of the Government sector. From a purely financial point of view, even including the capital account, a budgetary surplus position was reached in 1948 and was maintained throughout the rest of the period covered by the present discussion.

The main weakness which the country could not overcome on its own – and the same applied to most other Western European countries – lay in the sphere of the balance of payments, and more particularly in the dollar shortage. In the first half of 1948 this shortage became so acute that the reconstruction effort approached a serious breakdown for lack of the required imports from the dollar area. The Marshall Aid arrived just in time to continue and step up their supply, and its regional character multiplied its impact. Besides providing real resources for further expansion of production and exports, the U.S. aid contributed substantially to improving the financial performance of the Government on both the revenue and the expenditure side and to lowering the liquidity ratio, since most of the counterpart funds were sterilised or used for debt redemption. So, in 1949 there was little generation of new inflation and the opinion prevailed that there was 'no longer any question of an inflationary pressure of a serious nature' (Annual Report of the Netherlands Bank, 1949). Official monetary reserves started to rise.

The flare-up of inflation that occurred in 1950 was caused partly by the emergence of strong domestic demand following the abolition or liberalisation of consumption and import restrictions, partly by the effect of the currency realignment and the Korean crisis on the prices of imported goods. Anticipatory purchasing intensified the pressure of demand. Commercial bank credit expanded significantly, and large amounts of secondary liquidity were mobilized to assist in the financing of imports. Despite the cresting of Marshall Aid the balance of payments and the official reserve positions deteriorated to an unacceptable degree.

Once more strong corrective action was called for, but the reimposition of direct controls, except on less urgent investments, was refuted. In the early months of 1951 a comprehensive programme of disinflationary measures was introduced aiming at a reduction of effective demand; the programme was widespread and generally accepted as equitable. When soon thereafter the international inflationary storm subsided, the Netherlands economy emerged from it in both internal and external equilibrium. Already in 1952 the balance of payments showed a large surplus resulting in a much improved official reserve position.

In the early days of 1953 the Government of The Netherlands informed the Government of the United States that, on the strength of its economic and financial position, the country no longer needed to ask for aid.

GPSR Compliance

The European Union's (EU) General Product Safety Regulation (GPSR) is a set of rules that requires consumer products to be safe and our obligations to ensure this.

If you have any concerns about our products, you can contact us on ProductSafety@springernature.com

In case Publisher is established outside the EU, the EU authorized representative is:

Springer Nature Customer Service Center GmbH
Europaplatz 3
69115 Heidelberg, Germany

Batch number: 10830935

Printed by Printforce, the Netherlands